SCHIRMER'S LIBRARY
OF MUSICAL CLASSICS

FRIEDRICH SEITZ

Pupil's Concertos

For Violin and Piano

G. SCHIRMER, Inc.

DISTRIBUTED BY

HAL•LEONARD®
CORPORATION
7777 W. BLUEMOUND RD. P.O. BOX 13819 MILWAUKEE, WI 53213

Fifth Pupil's Concerto

for

Violin

Edited and fingered by
Philipp Mittell

Friedrich Seitz. Op. 22

Allegro moderato

Violin

Piano

Andante cantabile

Violin

SCHIRMER'S LIBRARY
OF MUSICAL CLASSICS

FRIEDRICH SEITZ

Pupil's Concertos

For Violin and Piano

G. SCHIRMER, Inc.

DISTRIBUTED BY

7777 W. BLUEMOUND RD. P.O. BOX 13819 MILWAUKEE, WI 53213

Fifth Pupil's Concerto

Edited and fingered by
Philipp Mittell

Violin

Friedrich Seitz. Op. 22

Violin

Violin

Violin

Rondò
Allegretto

Violin

Tempo I

Meno mosso